Healthy Fruit Smoothies

35 Low Calorie, Healthy Smoothies
Made With Your Favorite Fruits

By:

Lee Anne Dobbins

Table Of Contents

Introduction

What are healthy fruit smoothies?

Smoothies can be a great refreshing drink that is also healthy for you. But, you need to be careful about what you put into your smoothie because not all of them are good for you!

Just because a smoothie contains fruit, doesn't necessarily mean it is healthy. Sure, the fruit itself is healthy, but the other ingredients like sugar, ice cream and even milk can make the smoothie not so healthy.

That's why I've written this book with fruit smoothie recipes that include all healthy ingredients! And the best part is, because the ingredients are healthy - most of the smoothies are very low in calories with many of them being around only 200 calories per serving.

What To Put In Your Smoothie

Naturally, a good fruit smoothie is going to have lots of fruit! I usually like to keep bags of frozen fruit in my freezer so that I can whip up any smoothie I want at any time. This also helps to keep the fruit from going bad. The frozen fruits are good to use instead of ice cubes that can water down the smoothie.

You can mix other healthy things in with your fruit too. I love to use coconut and almond milk and you'll find those in a lot of these recipes. Low-fat greek yogurt is another healthy ingredient to mix in. And, of course you can add various herbs and spices as well as natural sweeteners like honey and agave nectar. Believe it or not, vegetables go great in fruit smoothies too!

You could also add some protein to your smoothie and make it into a complete meal. You can use protein powder or egg whites (either from real egg whites or the ones you can buy in the container at the store). For protein powder, I usually add just a half scoop of vanilla flavored protein and it doesn't seem to affect the taste at all. Egg whites wouldn't have any affect on taste either, but it might make your smoothie more liquidy so you might want to add another ice cube into the mix to make up for it.

I don't have egg whites or protein powder in any of the smoothies in this book, but quite a few of them use yogurt and almond milk which both have protein in them.

Smoothies Vs Juicing

A lot of people tout juicing as a healthy habit (which it is), but, in many ways, smoothies can be healthier than juices.

When you juice, you remove the pulp from the fruits and vegetables. Smoothies leave the pulp in, so you are getting all the beneficial fiber as well as vitamins and minerals. Fiber is important for heart health and helps to keep your digestive system regular. Most people don't get enough fiber in their diets and smoothies are a great way to get more of it without even realizing that you are!

Making Your Smoothies Even Healthier

Almost anything can be added to your smoothie and one way to make them really healthy is to add in some herbs and spices. Herbs and spices are nutritional powerhouses and contain healthy properties that can prevent and treat many illnesses. I have another book full of smoothie recipes using herbs and spices, but I wanted to talk about one special spice here and let you know an easy way to add it to any smoothie that you make.

That spice is turmeric. If you haven't heard about it, you should look it up. It's turning out to be somewhat of a miracle spice - it's loaded with antioxidants and is a powerful anti-inflammatory as well as antibacterial food.

Recently, turmeric is being studied for it's ability to destroy cancer cells and is also thought to help treat arthritis, reduce the risk of stroke and blood clots, as well as aid in liver health and digestive problems like IBS and even stomach ulcers.

Needless to say, adding more turmeric to your diet is good for you!

Normally, you would find turmeric in curries and other similar dishes. It has a very distinctive taste that many of you might not want to eat daily. I've found a way, though, to add it to my daily smoothies and I don't even taste it in the smoothie at all!

Here's what I do:

1. Put the smoothie ingredients in the blender as per the instructions.
2. Add in 1/8 - 1/4 teaspoon turmeric
3. Add in 1/4 teaspoon coconut oil
4. Add in 1/8 teaspoon black pepper

The coconut oil and black pepper are essential because they help your body absorb the healthy nutrients from the turmeric.

Then simply blend as instructed and drink! You won't even notice the turmeric was added and you'll be greatly increasing the health benefits of your smoothie!

Berry Orange Smoothie

Serves 2

This is a nice light smoothie, perfect for a snack or light breakfast. It's loaded with vitamin C and, since it's made with all fruit, it's very low in calories and fat.

Ingredients:

2 seedless oranges
1 cup frozen strawberries
1 cup frozen raspberries

Preparation:

Peel the oranges and remove most of the white pith.

Cut the oranges into quarters.

Put the oranges into the blender first, then the frozen fruit on top.

Blend until well mixed.

Nutritional Value:
Per Serving: 124 calories, 31g carbohydrates, 1g fat, 3g protein

Raspberry Coconut Smoothie

Serves 2

Raspberries are not only the most delicious berry, but they may help prevent cancer too! That's because they are high in ellagic acid which is a known cancer blocker and anti-carcinogen. Raspberries don't last very long in the fridge, so I like to keep a bag of them frozen in the freezer and that way I can indulge in a healthy raspberry smoothie whenever I want.

Ingredients:

2 cups raspberries
1 cup coconut milk
6 ice cubes (unless raspberries are frozen, then you only need a couple)
1 tablespoon honey

Preparation:

Put the coconut milk in the blender (I use Silk coconut milk which can be found in the Soy milk section at your grocery store).

Add the raspberries, ice cubes and honey.

Blend on high for about 20 seconds until smooth.

Nutritional Value:
Per Serving: 136 calories, 27g carbohydrates, 4g fat, 2g protein

Blueberry Honey Smoothie

Serves 2

This smoothie focuses on one fruit - Blueberries! That's because they are one of the healthiest foods around and contain a variety of vitamins and nutrients. The honey in the recipe will sweeten the tartness of the berries. Use local honey if you can - its better for you. If you have a problem with high blood sugar, then you might look at substituting agave nectar instead of the honey.

Ingredients:

1 1/2 cup frozen blueberries
4 ice cubes
1/2 cup nonfat vanilla yogurt
1 cup almond or coconut milk
3 tablespoons honey

Preparation:

Put the almond or coconut milk in the blender (I use Silk almond coconut milk blend - you can find it right in the soy milk section of most grocery stores).

Add the ice cubes, yogurt, berries and honey.

Blend until smooth.

Nutritional Value:
Per Serving: 237 calories, 55g carbohydrates, 2g fat, 7g protein

Pineapple Banana Mango Smoothie

Serves 2

This is one of my favorites because I love the smooth tropical flavor. The mango can be a bit difficult to cut up with a knife, but if you buy one of those mango corers it makes the job a lot easier. I keep the banana frozen in the freezer to make the smoothie even thicker.

Ingredients:

1 banana
1 1/2 cup fresh pineapple (don't use the canned stuff, buy a real one!)
1 cup mango
8 ice cubes

Preparation:

Add all ingredients to blender.

You may have to add in a little water if it gets too thick, just enough so it will blend.

Blend until smooth.

Nutritional Value:
Per Serving: 170 calories, 44g carbohydrates, 0g fat, 2g protein

Pineapple Banana Coconut Smoothie

Serves 2

Pineapple is loaded with anti-inflammatory properties and it makes a good skin exfoliator too. Just rub the inside of the "skin" that you cut off on your face and let it sit for a few minute then wash it off and see how good your skin feels!

Ingredients:

1 1/2 cup fresh pineapple
1 frozen banana
1 cup coconut milk
1/2 teaspoon vanilla extract
5 ice cubes

Preparation:

Add all ingredients to the blender and blend until smooth.

Add more vanilla to taste or some stevia to sweeten it if you like.

Nutritional Value:
Per Serving: 160 calories, 34g carbohydrates, 3g fat, 2g protein

Raspberry Lime Smoothie

Serves 2

One of my favorite drinks in the summer is a raspberry lime ricky. This is kind of a take-off on that but I've included some frozen coconut milk ice cream to make it creamier. Don't forget to sprinkle some raspberries on top and stick a sprig of mint leaves on the side of the glass.

Ingredients:

1 cup raspberries
1 cup coconut milk ice cream (if you can't find that, use frozen yogurt)
1 frozen banana
2 limes, peeled
8 mint leaves
5 ice cubes

Preparation:

Put the ice cream into the blender, then add the other ingredients on top of that. Depending on the type of blender you have, you may want to juice the limes first so that you don't get seeds in your drink. Blend until creamy.

Nutritional Value:
Per Serving: 265 calories, 49g carbohydrates, 9g fat, 3g protein

Cinnamon Apple Smoothie

Serves 2

Everyone knows that an apple a day keeps the doctor away and that's because apples have loads of vitamins and minerals. The perfect compliment to apples is cinnamon which is also pretty healthy for you - it can help regulate blood sugar, lower cholesterol, treat headaches, boost memory and has anti-fungal properties.

Ingredients:

2 apples, cored
1 1/2 cups coconut milk
1/4 teaspoon cinnamon
8 ice cubes

Preparation:

Put all the ingredients in the blender and blend until smooth.

You don't have to peel the apples if you have a high powered blender (there's lots of nutrients in the skin).

Nutritional Value:
Per Serving: 171 calories, 35g carbohydrates, 5g fat, 2g protein

Apple Carrot Smoothie

Serves 2

I love the combination of apples and carrots, they are delicious together and both provide a host of vitamins and minerals.   I've also included cucumber which gives the smoothie a crisps, fresh taste.

Ingredients:

1 apple, cored
1/2 cup apple sauce (natural, unsweetened)
1/2 cup carrots, peeled and sliced thin
1/2 cup cucumber
1/8 teaspoon cinnamon
8 ice cubes

Preparation:

Put all the ingredients in the blender and blend until smooth.

If your blender isn't very high powered you will want to be sure to cut the carrots very thin so you don't get any carrot "lumps" in your smoothie.

Nutritional Value:
Per Serving: 98 calories, 19g carbohydrates, 0g fat, 1g protein

Strawberry Banana Mint Smoothie

Serves 2

This fruit smoothie has a different twist with some mint leaves added! The mint not only adds to the taste, but mint is also a good source of vitamins A and C and can help soothe digestive disorders and respiratory problems. I you don't have mint on hand, you can substitute basil instead.

Ingredients:

1 cup strawberries
1 large banana
1 cup nonfat vanilla yogurt
6 mint leaves
1/4 teaspoon vanilla extract
8 ice cubes

Preparation:

Put all the ingredients in the blender and blend until smooth.

I usually break up the mint leaves with my fingers first to bring the flavorful oils to the surface.

Nutritional Value:
Per Serving: 178 calories, 36g carbohydrates, 0g fat, 10g protein

Watermelon Cantaloupe Smoothie

Serves 2

Melons are a great low calorie health food. Since they have a high water content, they have more vitamins and minerals per calorie than many foods and the abundance of water helps carry the nutrients to your cells quickly and efficiently. They are fat free and loaded with antioxidants and vitamins including Vitamin A, Vitamin C, Vitamin B6 and Vitamin B1. Watermelon has loads of lycopene which has recently been studied for it's role in preventing certain types of cancer.

Ingredients:

1 1/2 cup watermelon
1 1/2 cup cantaloupe
1 tablespoon honey
8 ice cubes

Preparation:

Put all the ingredients in the blender and blend until smooth.

For an added treat, stick some mint leaves on the side of the glass or add them to the blender with the melons.

Nutritional Value:
Per Serving: 112 calories, 29g carbohydrates, 0g fat, 2g protein

Cherry Raspberry Smoothie

Serves 2

Cherries are packed with antioxidants and are an excellent source of Vitamin A. They also have lots of Vitamins C and E as well as fiber, iron, folate, potassium and magnesium. They are said to help reduce inflammation and aid in brain health. Cherries are one of the few food sources of melatonin which helps regulate your sleep cycles.

Ingredients:

1 cup cherries, pitted
1 cup raspberries
1/2 cup low-fat vanilla yogurt
1 tablespoon honey
1/2 teaspoon vanilla extract
8 ice cubes

Preparation:

Put all the ingredients in the blender and mix until smooth.

Instead of vanilla extract, you might try adding in some vanilla bean which will have additional health benefits.

Nutritional Value:
Per Serving: 168 calories, 37g carbohydrates, 2g fat, 6g protein

Kiwi Grape Smoothie

Serves 2

Kiwis are loaded with Vitamin C and potassium, grapes provide lots of Vitamin A, Vitamin C, Vitamin B6 and folate making this smoothie a flavortul, nutritional powerhouse.

Ingredients:

1 1/2 cup grapes
1 cup kiwi, peeled
1 frozen banana
5 ice cubes

Preparation:

Put all ingredients in a blender and mix until smooth.

If you want, you can freeze the grapes beforehand but, if you do, you might have to add some water to the blender to get things going.

Nutritional Value:
Per Serving: 189 calories, 48g carbohydrates, 1g fat, 3g protein

Grapefruit Citrus Smoothie

Serves 2

One grapefruit provides 83% of your RDA of Vitamin C and 29% of Vitamin A. When combined with the other ingredients in this smoothie, you get all the vitamin C you need for the day, plus a host of other vitamins and minerals as well as lots of fiber.

Ingredients:

1 large grapefruit, peeled
1 orange, peeled
1 cup pineapple
1 cup mango
8 ice cubes

Preparation:

Put all the ingredients in a blender and mix until smooth.

Nutritional Value:
Per Serving: 156 calories, 40g carbohydrates, 0g fat, 2g protein

Peach Raspberry Smoothie

Serves 2

Peaches have lots of Vitamin A and Vitamin C and are loaded with antioxidants and fiber. A perfect fruit for a low calorie morning breakfast smoothie!

Ingredients:

4 peaches
1/2 cup raspberries
1 tablespoon honey
8 ice cubes

Preparation:

Cut up the peaches and remove the pits.

Keep the skin on since a lot of the vitamins are in the skin.

Put all the ingredients in the blender and blend until smooth.

Nutritional Value:
Per Serving: 171 calories, 42g carbohydrates, 1g fat, 4g protein

Pear Ginger Smoothie

Serves 2

The combination of pears, ginger and cinnamon in this smoothie make for great taste and great health. Pears are very high in fiber and have a decent amount of Vitamins C, A, K, B6, B3 and B2. Cinnamon can help lower blood sugar and cholesterol. Ginger can help soothe an upset stomach and has powerful anti-inflammatory benefits.

Ingredients:

2 pears, peeled and seeded
1 cup almond milk
1 tablespoon ginger, freshly grated
1/2 teaspoon cinnamon
8 ice cubes

Preparation:

Put all the ingredients in the blender and blend until smooth.

You can chop the pears and freeze them ahead of time if you want.

Nutritional Value:
Per Serving: 154 calories, 34g carbohydrates, 3g fat, 2g protein

Cantaloupe Strawberry Raspberry Smoothie

Serves 2

Cantaloupes are loaded with Vitamin A and are a good source of Vitamin K as well as the B vitamins. Strawberries and Raspberries have lots of Vitamin C and all the fruits in this mix, of course, are loaded with anti-oxidants and fiber.

Ingredients:

1/2 cantaloupe
1 cup strawberries
1 cup raspberries
8 ice cubes

Preparation:

Remove the rind from the cantaloupe and core the strawberries.

Put all the ingredients in the blender and mix until smooth.

Nutritional Value:
Per Serving: 126 calories, 30g carbohydrates, 1g fat, 3g protein

Melon Yogurt Smoothie

Serves 2

This smoothie combines honeydew melons and cantaloupe with yogurt for a light, creamy smoothie. Melons are loaded with vitamins and minerals, especially vitamin A. You can use any melons in this recipe and it will taste divine!

Ingredients:

1 cup honeydew melon
1 cup cantaloupe
1 cup low-fat vanilla yogurt
1/4 teaspoon vanilla extract
1/2 tablespoon honey
8 ice cubes

Preparation:

Put all the ingredients in the blender and mix until smooth.

Nutritional Value:
Per Serving: 190 calories, 36g carbohydrates, 2g fat, 10g protein

Banana Pineapple Smoothie

Serves 2

This smoothie is sweet and simple. I like to keep the bananas frozen in the fridge and use them to make the smoothie even colder. You might have to add some water to this one as it can tend to come out really thick.

Ingredients:

2 Large bananas
2 cups pineapple
8 ice cubes

Preparation:

Put all the ingredients in a blender and mix until smooth.

Nutritional Value:
Per Serving: 196 calories, 51g carbohydrates, 1g fat, 3g protein

Lemon Yogurt Smoothie

Serves 2

Lemon is one of the "feel good" foods that I have listed in my Mood Boosting foods book because it can actually help put you in a good mood! Not only that but its loaded with Vitamin C and has antibacterial properties as well as being a powerful antioxidant. So, the next time you are feeling down in the dumps, whip up one of these smoothies to pick up your mood!

Ingredients:

The juice of 4 lemons
2 cups low fat vanilla yogurt
1 banana
1 tablespoon honey
8 ice cubes

Preparation:

Put all the ingredients in the blender and blend until smooth.

If you really want a blast of lemon flavor, feel free to add some lemon zest, either into the smoothie or on top after you pour it into the glass.

Nutritional Value:

Per Serving: 363 calories, 76g carbohydrates, 4g fat, 11g protein

Plum Mango Watermelon Smoothie

Serves 2

Plums add a nice sweetness to any smoothie. Be sure to include the skin in your smoothie as that is where a lot of the vitamins are. Plums have Vitamin A, Vitamin C and Vitamin B2 as well as lots of fiber and antioxidants.

Ingredients:

2 plums, pit removed
1/2 mango
1 banana
2 cups watermelon
8 ice cubes

Preparation:

Put all the ingredients in the blender.

I usually put the watermelon in first because it Is more watery and will help to create enough liquid to gets things blended.

Nutritional Value:
Per Serving: 180 calories, 46g carbohydrates, 0g fat, 2g protein

Citrus Detox Smoothie

Serves 2

Citrus fruits are known for their detoxification properties and this smoothie has 3 of them - lemon, lime and orange. They are also loaded with fiber and, of course, Vitamin C as well as other vitamins and minerals. If you really want to detox, add some dandelion greens to your smoothie (just a few will help add to the cleansing properties of the drink and won't effect the taste too much).

Ingredients:

1 lemon (peeled)
1 lime (peeled)
2 oranges (peeled)
2 bananas, frozen
1/2 cup water

Preparation:

Squeeze the lemon and lime into the blender, taking care to not let any seeds get in.

You can squeeze them through a strainer or pick the seeds out of them and throw the fruit in.

Add the rest of the ingredients and blend until smooth.

Nutritional Value:
Per Serving: 206 calories, 54g carbohydrates, 1g fat, 3g protein

Peachy Creamy Smoothie with Watermelon

Serves 2

Peaches are a good source of Vitamins A, E, C, K and B6 as well as niacin, folate, riboflavin, thiamin and pantothenic acid. Watermelon is one of the best sources of lycopene which is thought to help reduce the risk of some types of cancers and is also a good source of potassium as well as other vitamins and minerals. This smoothie combines them both, along with other ingredients, for a powerfully healthy, and tasty drink.

Ingredients:

2 peaches
2 cups watermelon
1 cup vanilla low-fat yogurt
8 ice cubes

Preparation:

Put all the ingredients in a blender and blend until smooth.

Nutritional Value:
Per Serving: 217 calories, 43g carbohydrates, 3g fat, 12g protein

Melon Bash Smoothie

Serves 2

Melons are low in fat and calories but high in vitamins, minerals and fiber so they are a perfect health food for smoothies. This smoothie contains 3 different types of melons, but you can mix and match however you want - use 2 cups of cantaloupe and 1 cup of watermelon or all cantaloupe or 2 cups honeydew and 1 cup cantaloupe etc...

Ingredients:

1 cup honeydew melon
1 cup cantaloupe
1 cup watermelon
2 teaspoons fresh lime juice
8 ice cubes

Preparation:

Put the watermelon in the blender first, then add the other ingredients.

Blend until smooth.

If the ingredients aren't blending well, add a little bit of water to get them going.

Nutritional Value:
Per Serving: 85 calories, 21g carbohydrates, 0g
fat, 2g protein

Blueberry Smoothie

Serves 2

Blueberries are one of the most potent antioxidant foods and the good news is that freezing them does not affect the anthocyanin (antioxidants) so they are just as good for you frozen as they are fresh. I love to keep a big bag of them in my freezer so I can make blueberry smoothies whenever I want. Blueberries are high in fiber and Vitamin C and are low in calories - like most berries they are low GI foods so won't raise your blood sugar levels.

Ingredients:

1 1/2 cups frozen blueberries
1 frozen banana
1 cup almond, coconut or soy milk

Preparation:

Put all the ingredients in a blender and blend until smooth.

If you are using fresh berries instead of frozen, you will need to add a handful of ice cubes to get the smoothie to be thick.

Nutritional Value:
Per Serving: 153 calories, 36g carbohydrates, 2g fat, 2g protein

Grape Ape Smoothie

Serves 2

Grapes are a rich source of vitamins and minerals and have been used in natural medicine to treat indigestion, migraines, constipation, fatigue and even asthma. The red ones, especially, are loaded with flavonoids - powerful antioxidants. You can use red or green in this recipe, but make sure they are seedless as you won't want to be surprised by little seeds in your drink.

Ingredients:

2 cups grapes
1/2 cup low-fat vanilla yogurt
1/2 cup water
1 tablespoon honey
8 ice cubes

Preparation:

Put all the ingredients in a blender.

You can use fresh or frozen grapes - if you use frozen you'll only need to add 3 or 4 ice cubes.

Blend until smooth.

Nutritional Value:
Per Serving: 191 calories, 44g carbohydrates, 1g fat, 5g protein

Fruit Bowl Smoothie

Serves 2

This smoothie has a variety of different fruits in it for a unique taste. You'll get a diverse range of vitamins and minerals from these different fruits and its a good way to clean out the fruit bowl.

Ingredients:

1 cup strawberries
1 cup peaches
1 frozen banana
1 apple, cored and deseeded but with skin still on
3/4 cup coconut milk
9 ice cubes

Preparation:

Put all the ingredients in the blender and blend until smooth.

Nutritional Value:
Per Serving: 203 calories, 47g carbohydrates, 2g fat, 3g protein

Mood Boosting Smoothie

Serves 2

This smoothie contains 5 of the top mood boosting foods which have been shown to help elevate your mood by affecting the chemicals and hormones that your body produces. Bananas are loaded with potassium which helps keep you alert and also contain tryptophan which helps your brain produce seratonin that helps you relax. Studies have shown that simply smelling lemons improve your mood. Yogurt has the protein that helps to keep you alert. Honey can help your body release seratonin and walnuts have Omega 3 and Omega 6 fatty acids that your brain needs in order to function properly and keep you in a good mood.

Ingredients:

1 cup lowfat vanilla greek yogurt
2 frozen bananas
Juice of 1 lemon
1/2 teaspoon lemon zest
4 walnuts
1/2 cup water or soy milk
8 ice cubes

Preparation:

Pulverize the walnuts in a food processor until they are the consistency of powder (you don't want walnut chunks in your smoothie!)

Put all the ingredients in a blender and blend until smooth.

Nutritional Value:

Per Serving: 329 calories, 55g carbohydrates, 10g fat, 14g protein

Papaya Ginger Stomach Soothing Smoothie

Serves 2

This smoothie has papaya and ginger which are known to help sooth an upset tummy. Papaya is also loaded with vitamins A, C and E as well as folate. Ginger root is a powerful antioxidant and antibacterial herb that has long been used to treat stomach issues, prevent colds and flu, relieve migraines and reduce inflammation.

Ingredients:

2 cups papaya
1 frozen banana
1/2 cup frozen strawberries
1 tablespoon freshly grated ginger root
1 tablespoon honey

Preparation:

Put all ingredients in a blender starting with the papaya first.

Blend until smooth. You may need to add a little water to get things started.

Nutritional Value:
Per Serving: 161 calories, 41g carbohydrates, 0g fat, 2g protein

Spicy Banana Coconut Smoothie

Serves 2

This smoothie has the creamy soothing base of bananas and coconut and the spicy zest of the warming spices - cinnamon, nutmeg and ginger. Loaded with anti-oxidants, vitamins and minerals, this smoothie can help reduce inflammation, lower blood sugar levels and treat an upset stomach as well as a host of other ailments.

Ingredients:

2 frozen bananas
2 cups light coconut milk
1/2 teaspoon cinnamon
1/2 teaspoon freshly grated ginger root
1/4 teaspoon nutmeg
1/4 teaspoon vanilla extract

Preparation:

Put all ingredients in a blender and blend until smooth.

If you prefer your smoothies really thick and cold, you might want to add some ice cubes to this one.

Nutritional Value:
Per Serving: 201 calories, 38g carbohydrates, 7g fat, 2g protein

Grape Green Tea Smoothie

Serves 2

This smoothie packs a powerful anti-oxidant punch with the combination of two ingredients loaded with antioxidants - grapes and green tea.

Ingredients:

2 cups frozen green seedless grapes
1 1/2 cups fresh brewed green tea, chilled
1 tablespoon honey or agave nectar

Preparation:

Put all ingredients in a blender and blend until smooth.

The agave nectar will give the smoothie a more "molasses" like taste than the honey, but agave nectar is lower on the glycemic index so it won't raise your blood sugar levels as much as honey will. That being said, either one is a healthier option over table sugar.

Nutritional Value:
Per Serving: 94 calories, 25g carbohydrates, 1g fat, 1g protein

Energizing Fruit Smoothie

Serves 2

This smoothie recipe is loaded with fruits that can help increase your energy. Bananas have been used by body builders for ages because of their high levels of potassium that help your muscles function. Watermelon is very hydrating due to its high water content and also has lots of B vitamins which help boost your energy. Blueberries are a superfood that can help improve brain function and yogurt has the protein and amino acids that help get rid of that sluggish feeling.

Ingredients:

1 frozen banana
2 cups watermelon
1 cup frozen blueberries
1 cup low-fat vanilla greek yogurt

Preparation:

Combine all ingredients in a blender and blend until smooth.

If you like your smoothies a little sweeter, you can add some agave nectar or honey.

Nutritional Value:
Per Serving: 208 calories, 42g carbohydrates, 0g fat, 13g protein

Memory Boosting Smoothie

Serves 2

Do you need a memory boost? Drinking this smoothie regularly can help you retain more information and boost your cognitive brain functions. It contains some of the best "brain boosting" foods including blueberries that are loaded with flavonoids which help with learning and memory, banana which help your body produce seratonin to elevate your mood and flax seeds that have Omega 6 and Omega 3 fatty acids which are vital for brain health.

Ingredients:

1 cup frozen blueberries
1/2 cup frozen raspberries
1 banana
1 cup low-fat greek yogurt
2 tablespoons freshly ground flax seeds

Preparation:

Put all ingredients in a blender and blend until smooth.

You might find the taste of this to be a little bland, and if you do, experiment with adding a little vanilla extract and honey to sweeten it up.

Nutritional Value:
Per Serving: 223 calories, 37g carbohydrates, 4g fat, 15g protein

Sweet and Salty Smoothie

Serves 2

The combination of Pineapple and celery in this smoothie is a very unique, tropical taste. This smoothie is a great detoxifying and anti-inflammatory drink with lots of vitamin C.

Ingredients:

2 cups chopped pineapple
1 banana
8 celery stalks
8 ice cubes

Preparation:

Put all the ingredients in the blender and blend until smooth.

You can add more or less celery to taste. If you want it more salty, add more celery stalks, less salty add less celery or more pineapple.

Nutritional Value:
Per Serving: 155 calories, 39g carbohydrates, 0g fat, 2g protein

Sour Green Apple Smoothie

Serves 2

Apples are a great low calorie food that are loaded with fiber and are thought to help keep your bones strong, lessen asthma attacks, manage diabetes and reduce the risk of certain types of cancer.

Ingredients:

2 green apples (I use granny smith), cored and seeded
1 frozen banana
1 cup frozen grapes
1 cup low fat vanilla greek yogurt

Preparation:

Put all ingredients in a blender and blend until smooth. If you want to sweeten it up a bit, you can add about a tablespoon of honey.

Nutritional Value:
Per Serving: 332 calories, 74g carbohydrates, 2g fat, 11g protein

Cold Fighting Smoothie

Serves 2

This smoothie is loaded with Vitamin C that can help lessen the severity of a cold. It also includes ginger that has mild pain relieving properties and has been shown in studies to fight certain types of viruses.

Ingredients:

1 cup pineapple
2 oranges
1/2 cup frozen strawberries
1 teaspoon freshly grated ginger root
1/2 teaspoon cayenne pepper (optional)
4 ice cubes

Preparation:

Put all ingredients in a blender and blend until smooth.

You may, or may not, like the addition of the cayenne pepper but if you are stuffed up the capsaicin in the cayenne pepper is a wonderful decongestant.

Nutritional Value:
Per Serving: 120 calories, 31g carbohydrates, 0g fat, 3g protein

About The Author

Lee Dobbins writes about healthy foods and simple ways to eat healthier. She would love to connect with you on her blog, Facebook or Twitter:

Blog - http://www.healingfoodscookbooks.com

Facebook - http://www.facebook.com/ healingfoodsbooks

Twitter - http://www.twitter.com/healingfoodscb

And don't forget to pick up her other books on smoothies and healthy eating:

Healing Herbs & Spices: Health Benefits of Popular Herbs & Spices Plus Over 70 Recipes To Use Them In

Healthy Smoothie Recipes - Healthy Herbal Smoothies That Are Nutritious, Delicious and Easy to Make

Made in the USA
Lexington, KY
19 December 2013